Original title:
The Recipe for Remarkable Relationships

Copyright © 2024 Swan Charm
All rights reserved.

Author: Paula Raudsepp
ISBN HARDBACK: 978-9916-86-764-8
ISBN PAPERBACK: 978-9916-86-765-5
ISBN EBOOK: 978-9916-86-766-2

Shared Plates and Dreams

In twilight's glow, we gather near,
With laughter's sound, our hearts sincere.
A table set with joy and cheer,
Each bite a story we hold dear.

The silverware of memories,
Reflects the warmth of shared histories.
We pass the dishes, complete the pleas,
In every taste, a soft reprise.

The aroma dances, spices blend,
In every forkful, hearts we mend.
As dreams unfold, our lives extend,
Around this table, love we send.

We savor moments, lost in time,
With every dish, our spirits climb.
Through shared plates, our hopes align,
Together we weave a dream divine.

So let us feast beneath the stars,
Forget our worries, heal our scars.
In shared plates, we find who we are,
A tapestry of love, not far.

Cuppa Companionship

In morning light, we share a brew,
Two cups, warm hearts, just me and you.
Steam rises high, whispers in air,
In this moment, nothing else compares.

Laughter pours in, like the coffee flows,
Each sip a memory, our comfort grows.
With every taste, stories unfold,
Cuppa companionship, worth more than gold.

Entwined Flavors

A pinch of spice, a hint of sweet,
Together we stir, a dance, a treat.
Herbs and citrus, flavors unite,
In harmony, they spark delight.

Chopping garlic, the scent ignites,
With every layer, the dish excites.
Entwined flavors, a symphony,
In each mouthful, a shared journey.

Toasting to Timelessness

Raise your glass, let the laughter soar,
In this moment, we cherish more.
Time stands still as we celebrate,
Memories linger, they captivate.

Each clink resounds with heartfelt cheer,
Toasting to love that we hold dear.
Timelessness wrapped in a shared gaze,
In this magic, we set ablaze.

Simplicity in Sharing

A loaf of bread, a humble spread,
In quiet moments, nothing is said.
Together we feast, no need for grand,
Just simple joys, hand in hand.

Fruit on the table, kindness abound,
In this giving, true love is found.
Simplicity shines, beneath the stars,
In every bite, no need for bars.

Beneath the Layered Heart

Beneath the layers, secrets lie,
Tender whispers, a gentle sigh.
Love's cocoon, warm and wide,
In the stillness, hearts confide.

Each layer peeled, revealing light,
Moments cherished, pure delight.
Through the shadows, truths emerge,
In every heartbeat, love's urge.

Whisking Bonds in Gentle Whirl

In the kitchen, laughter blends,
Whisking joy as love transcends.
A pinch of this, a splash of cheer,
Stirring memories, always near.

Flavors mixing, spices dance,
In every taste, a chance romance.
Connecting hearts in simple ways,
Whisking bonds through rainy days.

Flavors of Trust and Time

Time unfolds like a rich tapestry,
Each moment savored, a symphony.
Flavors of trust, sweet and rare,
Carried softly on the air.

With every tick, the heart expands,
Building dreams with gentle hands.
Layered stories, rich and bold,
In each bite, a love retold.

A Dash of Kindness

A dash of kindness, a sprinkle of care,
Transforming moments, everywhere.
Small acts of warmth, soft and bright,
Lightening burdens, bringing light.

In whispered words, compassion flows,
Seeds of goodwill, always grow.
With open hearts, we pave the way,
For brighter tomorrows, come what may.

A Pinch of Patience

A pinch of patience, time's gentle friend,
In the chaos, some guidelines to lend.
Waiting for blooms to unfold,
Trusting the journey, stories told.

With quiet strength, we hold our ground,
In still waters, wisdom is found.
A sprinkle of grace in each sigh,
Patience teaches us to fly.

Soulful Companionship

In quiet corners, we find peace,
Whispers of warmth that never cease.
Through laughter and tears, hand in hand,
Together we walk, a trust so grand.

Eyes that speak, hearts that share,
In the silence, love is laid bare.
Days turn to nights, still we remain,
Bound by the joy and the pain.

Memories woven like threads of gold,
Stories of heartbeats forever told.
In each moment, a treasure we see,
Soulful companionship, you and me.

Cooking Up Connection

In the kitchen, laughter brews,
Chopping veggies and sharing views.
Spices dance and flavors blend,
Creating dishes that never end.

A simmering pot, a shared delight,
Warm aromas fill the night.
With every stir, our hearts align,
Cooking up connection, so divine.

Taste the joy in every bite,
A feast of love under the light.
As we gather, our souls ignite,
In this moment, all feels right.

A Mix of Joy and Sorrow

In shadows cast, a light will gleam,
We dance through life, a fragile dream.
Each heartbeat holds both joy and pain,
A mix of sunshine, a touch of rain.

Through winding paths, we find our way,
In sorrow's grip, hope finds its sway.
Lessons learned in every scar,
Together we shine, no matter how far.

In laughter's echo, tears may fall,
Yet in our bond, we conquer all.
Embracing both, we rise and soar,
For it's the mix that we adore.

Sweet Moments of Togetherness

As daylight fades, we sit and sigh,
In the hush of dusk, time slips by.
Cup of tea and tales to tell,
Sweet moments linger, all is well.

Hands entwined, we watch the stars,
Counting dreams, no wish is far.
In silence shared, a bond so true,
Sweet moments blossom, me and you.

With every smile and gentle gaze,
In this warmth, we find our ways.
To cherish love, our hearts confess,
Sweet moments of togetherness.

Chopping Barriers

With every slice, we break the walls,
Unraveling fears that time recalls.
The knife of truth, so sharp and clear,
Cuts through doubt, brings us near.

We stand together, hand in hand,
No more divides, we make our stand.
In unity's light, we rise anew,
Chopping barriers, me and you.

Slicing Doubts

With steady hands, we take the knife,
Slicing doubts that strangle life.
Each cut reveals our greater dream,
Cleansing fears like a flowing stream.

Let's cut the noise that fills our heads,
And nourish hope where sorrow treads.
Slicing doubts, we find our way,
Embracing light with each new day.

Seasoning with Sincerity

Sprinkled truths like salt and spice,
Seasoning life, we pay the price.
With honesty, our flavors bold,
Creating bonds worth more than gold.

A dash of warmth, a pinch of care,
Saturating hearts, a love we share.
In every moment, let's be real,
Seasoning with sincerity, we heal.

The Flavorful Dance of Discourse

Words like rhythms, flowing free,
In vibrant tones, we start to see.
A flavorful dance, where voices blend,
Creating harmony, not just pretend.

With every step, we find our groove,
In the circle, we start to move.
The dance of discourse, alive and bright,
Illuminates the darkest night.

Harvest of Forgiveness and Growth

In fields of time, we plant the seeds,
Of forgiveness, to meet our needs.
Nurtured by love, neglected no more,
A harvest awaits, an open door.

As we gather, hearts swell with grace,
Harvesting lessons time can't erase.
Forgiveness blooms, growth intertwines,
In the garden of life, love shines.

The Sweetness of Forgiveness

In the deep well of the heart,
A whisper soft and low,
Where grudges fade like shadows,
And love begins to grow.

A gentle touch of kindness,
A warming of the soul,
Forgiveness breathes its magic,
And makes the broken whole.

Let go of heavy burdens,
Release the bitter strife,
In the sweet embrace of healing,
We find the joy of life.

With open hearts, we gather,
The past becomes a breeze,
And every step together,
Brings hope and inner peace.

So cherish all the moments,
Both simple and profound,
For in the art of forgiving,
True freedom can be found.

Garnished with Grins

When laughter fills the silence,
And joy dances on air,
Each moment shared a treasure,
A gift that we both share.

With playful sparks igniting,
And smiles that warmly shine,
We garnish every heartbeat,
With love that's truly divine.

In the simple everyday,
Where giggles intertwine,
We find our greatest blessings,
In moments, yours and mine.

As sunlight paints the morning,
And stars light up the night,
Our hearts blend in the laughter,
Creating pure delight.

So let's keep on creating,
With memories in full bloom,
For life is best garnished,
With grins that chase the gloom.

Nourishment in Vulnerability

In the quiet of confession,
Where whispers find their flight,
We shed the weight of silence,
And step into the light.

To open up our chambers,
And share our hidden scars,
Is to nourish soul connections,
And reach for shining stars.

Though fear may grip the heartstrings,
And doubt may cloud the mind,
In vulnerability's embrace,
True strength we often find.

For when we show our real selves,
And let the guard fall down,
We cultivate a garden,
Where trust and love abound.

So let us share our stories,
With honesty and grace,
For in the act of being real,
We find our sacred space.

A Hearth of Togetherness

Gathered 'round the glowing fire,
Where warmth and laughter blend,
We share our tales and dreams,
In the arms of family and friend.

The flickering flames remind us,
Of moments rich and bright,
As hearts connect and mingle,
In the comforting, soft light.

Each crackle holds a memory,
A treasure to embrace,
In this hearth of togetherness,
We find our special place.

With every shared adventure,
And every word of cheer,
We weave a bond unbroken,
That draws us ever near.

So let the fire keep burning,
And let our spirits soar,
For in this heart of togetherness,
We find forevermore.

Cooking Up Compromise

In the kitchen, aromas blend,
Ingredients mix, hands extend.
A dash of patience, a sprinkle of care,
Together we simmer, together we share.

Stirring the pot of differing views,
Finding the flavor that both can choose.
With every taste, we adjust the heat,
Creating a dish that's savory and sweet.

On the table, we gather 'round,
Every voice heard, harmony found.
Forks clink softly, laughter does rise,
In the warmth of the meal, understanding lies.

As we feast on the fruits of our toil,
The seeds of respect begin to spoil.
Flavorful moments, a recipe bright,
In cooking up compromise, we see the light.

A Gentle Boil of Empathy

In the pot, the water waits,
Slowly rising, embracing fates.
Gentle bubbles, softly they rise,
A dance of patience beneath the skies.

Each drop a story, silently shared,
Of laughter, sorrow; hearts laid bare.
The heat can soften, can also burn,
In this gentle boil, we all learn.

Stirring thoughts with tender grace,
Finding warmth in every face.
For each ingredient adds its part,
Bubbling kindness, a work of heart.

From the simmer, we gain insight,
Through shared warmth, wrong turns feel right.
In the pot, we find our way,
Empathy brews, brightening the day.

Coursing Through Our Hearts

Like rivers flowing, hearts align,
Winding paths where souls entwine.
Each gentle current sings its song,
In this vast ocean, we all belong.

Water reflects the sun above,
Mirroring kindness, deep as love.
Nurtured by trust, we journey wide,
With every ripple, we feel the tide.

Together we paddle, side by side,
Through winding channels, we take pride.
With every stroke, our spirits soar,
Coursing through hearts, forevermore.

In the depths, we find our peace,
A tranquil rhythm where worries cease.
Sharing the voyage, we navigate,
In the flow of compassion, we celebrate.

Batter of Trust

Mixing the flour, blending so fine,
Adding the sugar, a taste divine.
In the bowl of our hearts, things unite,
Creating a batter, fluffy and light.

Beating the eggs with a splash of care,
Each fold together, a bond we share.
A pinch of belief, a stir of the soul,
With every turn, we make each other whole.

Pouring the batter into the pan,
Knowing together, we'll make a stand.
As it rises, we watch and cheer,
Trust baked deeply, year after year.

Cooling the layer, an icing to spread,
Crafting our futures, together we're led.
In this recipe, our hopes combine,
Batter of trust, forever we dine.

Icing of Respect

On a canvas of cake, the icing pours,
Layers of friendship, love that soars.
Whipped with care, so smooth and sweet,
In each delicate swirl, our hearts meet.

Colors of kindness, each hue unique,
Adding dimension, in every peak.
Adorning our lives with patience and grace,
Icing of respect, a warm embrace.

As we savor the taste of this treat,
Every bite blissful, oh so complete.
Together we celebrate, laughter runs free,
In the sweetness of moments, just you and me.

Though life can be crumbly, a slice of delight,
With icing of respect, each day feels right.
Sharing our stories, we take the chance,
In this cake of life, forever we dance.

Love's Secret Flavor

In the quiet whispers of the night,
Sweet aromas drift, taking flight.
A tender touch and a knowing gaze,
In love's embrace, we find our ways.

With every glance, a spark ignites,
Hearts entwined in soft moonlight.
A savory kiss beneath the trees,
Love's secret flavor floats on the breeze.

In kitchens warm with gentle heat,
We stir our passions, bittersweet.
Each recipe a story shared,
In every bite, how much we cared.

Time slows down in this sacred space,
Two souls dance in a warm embrace.
Tasting dreams in every bite,
Love's secret flavor, pure delight.

Together we weave a tapestry fine,
A blend of scents, a taste of time.
Hand in hand, we explore and savor,
In every meal, love's secret flavor.

Trust: The Essential Spice

In the heart of a bustling kitchen,
Trust simmers, slowly, without condition.
With each chopped herb, a promise made,
In the warmth of friendship, fears soon fade.

Like salt that enhances every dish,
Without it, flavors can't truly flourish.
A bond formed through laughter and tears,
In the rich broth of shared hopes and fears.

Through trials and tests, we stand strong,
Together, we find where we belong.
In every stir we share our fate,
Trust is the spice that cannot wait.

A dash of faith, a sprinkle of truth,
In the recipe forged since our youth.
Ingredients blend, creating a feast,
Trust, the essential spice, never least.

As we share meals and dreams anew,
We taste the love in all that we do.
In this kitchen of life, side by side,
Trust is the flavor that will never hide.

Conversations Under the Stars

Beneath a sky of twinkling lights,
We share our dreams on quiet nights.
With every word, a spark ignites,
In whispered hopes, our future brightens.

The moon overhead casts silver beams,
We speak of love and of distant dreams.
Each moment cherished, precious and rare,
Conversations deep, the world laid bare.

In the stillness, time drifts away,
In laughter and silence, we find our way.
With every glance, we understand,
In the quiet wonder, we join hand in hand.

Stars above our heads like jewels glow,
Reflecting the feelings we both know.
Through stories shared, our hearts connect,
Conversations woven with deep respect.

As the night fades into a soft dawn,
We carry the whispers of love reborn.
These moments cherished, forever ours,
In conversations held under the stars.

Harmony in a Chaotic Kitchen

In the kitchen where flavors collide,
Chaos reigns, yet joy won't hide.
Pots clank and laughter fills the air,
In this sweet mess, love's everywhere.

Chopping and stirring, we dance around,
With every heartbeat, a joyful sound.
Spices mingle, the rhythm flows,
In this delightful chaos, love grows.

Recipes shared, improvisation bright,
Together we blend, creating delight.
The essence of home in every bite,
Harmony thrives, transforming the night.

In flour clouds and smiles galore,
We savor the joy of a feast in store.
With passion and purpose, we create,
Culinary magic on each plate.

Though chaos swirls, we stand as one,
In this sacred space, our journey's begun.
With every dish, our hearts entwined,
Harmony reigns, beautifully blind.

The Art of Listening

In silence, we find the truth,
The heart speaks loud and clear.
With open ears and gentle grace,
    We draw the world near.

Each whisper tells a story bright,
    A tale of joy or strife.
With patience, we hold every word,
    An echo of life.

The pause between the breaths we share,
    Holds secrets in the air.
    To truly hear is a gift we give,
    A bond beyond compare.

With each shared thought, we canvas dreams,
    Painted on wisdom's hue.
    In listening, we build the bridge,
    Connecting me to you.

So let us cherish every voice,
    In laughter or in tears.
The art of listening lays the path
    To love that perseveres.

A Pinch of Adventure

Step outside your comfort zone,
Embrace the unknown's call.
A pinch of thrill, a dash of risk,
Let spontaneity enthrall.

The world has wonders yet to see,
In mountains high and low.
With every trail we dare to tread,
Our spirits freely flow.

In little things, adventure waits,
A sunset's vibrant hue.
In laughter shared with open hearts,
The new feels bright and true.

So take the leap into the wild,
With courage as your guide.
Every journey spins a tale,
Where memories abide.

A pinch of adventure fuels the soul,
With each new path we find.
Together, we'll chase the fleeting joy,
And leave the past behind.

Infusing Life with Love

In gestures kind, we share the light,
A touch, a smile, a word.
Infusing life with love so pure,
A symphony unheard.

The warmth of hearts that intertwine,
Creates a gentle spark.
With every moment, every sigh,
We write our own trademark.

Through trials faced and laughter found,
Love thrives in every scene.
It lifts us high and grounds us firm,
An anchor in between.

In whispered hopes and tender dreams,
We weave our lives as one.
Infusing life with love's embrace,
We'll shine just like the sun.

So let love be our guiding force,
As seasons come and go.
In every heartbeat, every breath,
Together, we will grow.

Flavorful Companionship

In shared meals, stories unfold,
A feast for heart and mind.
With spices rare and laughter rich,
Companionship aligned.

Each flavor tells a tale profound,
Of cultures meeting here.
In every bite, a memory stirs,
That brings us ever near.

From sweet to bitter, bold to bland,
We savor every taste.
Together, we craft our recipes,
In moments never waste.

With tables set and candles lit,
We gather, warm and bright.
In flavorful companionship,
Each gathering's delight.

So raise a glass to those we love,
In joy and gratitude.
Flavorful moments linger long,
In friendship's sweet pursuit.

Tasting Life Together

In the kitchen, laughter flows,
Spices mingle, love it sows.
With each bite, stories shared,
Every meal shows we cared.

A sip of wine, a gentle tease,
Moments linger like the breeze.
Hands entwined, the table set,
In this life, no regrets yet.

Sunset colors paint the sky,
With each taste, we soar high.
Together, we create and dream,
Life's a savory, sweet theme.

Shared desserts, a wink, a smile,
Time stands still, just for a while.
In flavors bright, our hearts align,
Tasting life, your hand in mine.

Nurtured Bonds

In the garden, roots run deep,
We plant the seeds, our love to keep.
With each sunrise, hope will bloom,
Nurtured bonds, dispelling gloom.

Through the seasons, we will grow,
Watering dreams with gentle flow.
Fertilized by trust and care,
A testament to love we share.

In the autumn, leaves may fall,
Yet together, we stand tall.
Through the storms, we seek the light,
In each struggle, hearts unite.

As blossoms fade, new buds appear,
With every change, we persevere.
In nature's hold, our spirits thrive,
In nurturing, our love's alive.

Mixing Hearts with Harmony

In melodies, our souls collide,
With rhythms sweet, we can't divide.
Each note a promise, soft and true,
Harmonies found in me and you.

Dancing lightly, we take the stage,
In the spotlight, we turn the page.
With every beat, we share our song,
With each refrain, we grow more strong.

A symphony of laughter rings,
In this life, love's the song we sing.
Together we weave a perfect tune,
Under the stars, beneath the moon.

Chords entwined, forever bound,
In every silence, love is found.
With open hearts, we play our role,
Mixing hearts, we become whole.

The Tender Balance

In the dance of give and take,
We find the steps that love can make.
With every breath, we learn to sway,
In tender balance, night and day.

Holding tight yet letting go,
In this rhythm, our feelings flow.
Through gentle words and soft embrace,
We find our home, our sacred space.

With every challenge, we align,
In trust and patience, hearts entwine.
Together facing trials anew,
In balance, we're stronger, me and you.

As seasons change and shadows grow,
We walk the line, our love in tow.
In harmony, we shall expand,
The tender balance, hand in hand.

A Feast of Forged Connections

In the heart of laughter, we connect,
With stories shared, our spirits reflect.
Around the table, the warmth does grow,
Each moment crafted, like art in flow.

Friendships deepen with the passing days,
Through all the challenges, love always stays.
We gather close, no need for disguise,
In every glance, the bond never lies.

With every bite, we taste the trust,
In every cheer, a quiet must.
The feast we share, a sacred rite,
In this woven tapestry, we ignite.

Time's gentle hands shape our delight,
Building connections, oh so bright.
In the echoes of laughter, we find our place,
A cherished connection, wrapped in grace.

So here's to the moments, both big and small,
To the joys and sorrows, we embrace them all.
At this feast of hearts, we choose to believe,
In the power of connection, we weave and cleave.

Layers of Love and Life

Beneath the surface, we find our ties,
In layers of love, the heart never lies.
Each layer peeled reveals a story,
In the tapestry of life, all in glory.

Moments stacked like pages in a book,
With every glance, every gentle look.
Love intertwined, both fragile and bold,
In the silence, true feelings unfold.

A garden of memories, rich and deep,
In every corner, secrets we keep.
Through laughter and tears, we stitch our fate,
In layers of time, we cultivate.

As seasons change, our roots grow strong,
In the symphony of life, we sing along.
Through trials and triumphs, hand in hand,
Together we'll rise, together we stand.

So let us celebrate each layer we find,
In the journey of love, intertwined.
For in every fold, there's beauty to see,
In the layers of life, just you and me.

The Nourishment of Time Together

In gentle moments, we find our peace,
As time flows soft, our worries cease.
With each shared laugh, our burdens lighten,
In the quiet hours, our souls brighten.

Together we wander, through fields and dreams,
In the tapestry of time, we're stitched at the seams.
Every heartbeat echoes a cherished tune,
As we dance beneath the silver moon.

Cups of warmth held in tender hands,
Filled with whispers of far-off lands.
As the world outside fades to gray,
Our little sanctuary lights the way.

The nourishment of time, a sacred gift,
In the stillness, our spirits drift.
Moments unfold like petals in bloom,
Filling our hearts, erasing the gloom.

So here's to the hours, both sparse and grand,
In this journey of life, hand in hand.
For in every second, we forge and we tether,
In the warmth of our bond, we find true treasure.

Glaze of Gratitude

A sprinkle of thanks in the morning light,
Transforms ordinary into pure delight.
In each simple gesture, we softly find,
The glaze of gratitude, forever entwined.

For moments shared on this winding road,
In every word, love's sweet ode.
Through trials faced and battles won,
Our hearts unite as one, we become.

With every sunset painting the sky,
We reflect on the blessings that never die.
In laughter's embrace and in tears we shed,
The glaze of gratitude is lovingly spread.

As seasons change and time slips away,
In each fleeting moment, we choose to stay.
With every heartbeat, we sing our grace,
In the tapestry woven, we find our place.

So raise a glass to the love we share,
To the beauty of life, tender and rare.
In the glaze of gratitude, our spirits soar,
In the bonds we cherish, we seek no more.

Simmering in Shared Silence

In the quiet, we find peace,
Words unspoken, hearts release.
Time stands still, a gentle pause,
In this silence, we find cause.

Memories linger in the air,
Each breath echoes, a whispered prayer.
Together we sit, letting go,
In the simmering, our true selves flow.

Eyes meet softly, a knowing glance,
In this stillness, we take a chance.
No need for noise, just the trust,
In our silence, we must.

The world outside fades away,
In shared moments, we choose to stay.
Laughter muted, but hearts align,
In this silence, everything's fine.

As we linger, the warmth grows,
In shared silence, our bond shows.
No need for words, we've made our home,
In this quiet, we're never alone.

The Sweetness of Support

In the shadows, you stand tall,
A gentle hand when I might fall.
With every word, you lift me high,
In your presence, I learn to fly.

Through the storms, you are my calm,
Whispered strength, a healing balm.
With each smile, you light the way,
In your embrace, I find my stay.

When the world feels heavy, dark,
You remind me of my spark.
Together we rise, we face the tide,
In your support, I confide.

Every struggle, we brave together,
In your love, there's always weather.
A bond so sweet, it blooms and grows,
In your trust, my heart knows.

Through laughter and tears, we weave our fate,
In this journey, it's never too late.
With every hug, every shared dream,
The sweetness of support, like a steady stream.

A Table Set for Two

In the glow of candlelight,
Two plates wait, a simple sight.
With every dish, a story told,
In their warmth, our hearts unfold.

Forks and knives in perfect sync,
Each bite savored, think and link.
We share our dreams, our fears laid bare,
At this table, love fills the air.

The clink of glasses, a toast we share,
To moments cherished, to dreams we dare.
With laughter echoing, time stands still,
In each other's company, we find our will.

The world outside fades from view,
At this table set for two.
No need for fancy, no need for grand,
Just you and me, hand in hand.

As the night deepens, we hold on tight,
In our little haven, pure delight.
With every bite, we gather more,
A table set for two, opens door.

Blending Lives, Crafting Joy

In this dance of hearts entwined,
Two lives blend, a love combined.
Laughter echoes, shadows fade,
In this crafting, memories are laid.

With every day, we sketch anew,
In colors bright, in shades of blue.
Through playful moments, through the strife,
We carve our path, embracing life.

Each shared dream, a brush we wield,
In this canvas, our joy is revealed.
As we paint our days in hues of light,
Together, we make the dark turn bright.

In sunsets watched, and stars that glow,
We find our rhythm, our hearts in flow.
With gentle hands, we work as one,
In blending lives, our journey's begun.

Through every season, hand in hand,
We build our future, a promised land.
In crafting joy, together we sing,
In this dance of love, our hearts take wing.

Embracing Life's Ingredients

In the bowl of morning light,
We gather dreams and hopes so bright.
Mixing joy with a sprinkle of tears,
Each flavor tells of our years.

A dash of laughter, a pinch of grace,
These ingredients give life its pace.
Stirred with stories, memories in tow,
In this recipe, our spirits grow.

We whisk away worries, blend in delight,
Creating a feast from the heart of the night.
With every taste, we find our way,
Embracing life, come what may.

So gather your flavors, let colors unite,
From bitter to sweet, all seem just right.
For in every bite, we find our song,
A symphony of life, where we all belong.

Let's savor the moments, both big and small,
Each flavorful journey, we will recall.
With open hearts, let's take each chance,
For embracing life is a wondrous dance.

Sweeten the Difficult Days

When clouds hang low and shadows play,
We search for the light in a cloudy gray.
A sweetness found in the thorns so sharp,
In the stillness, we hear a lark.

A spoonful of kindness, a cup of care,
Adding warmth in the chill of despair.
Sprinkling hope like sugar on pain,
Transforming our doubt into joy once again.

In moments tough, let laughter rise,
Find the sunshine 'neath stormy skies.
With each setback, we learn to bend,
Sweetening trials with love we send.

The recipe for peace is simple, you see,
Mix patience with faith, let love be the key.
As we navigate storms and toughened ways,
We find strength to sweeten our difficult days.

So let's raise our glasses, toast to the fight,
With hearts intertwined, we'll cherish the light.
Through challenges met, our spirits remain,
In this kitchen of life, love conquers pain.

Stirring with Purpose

In the pot of dreams, we stir with grace,
Mixing intention in every space.
With hands steady, we gather our might,
Crafting a future that feels just right.

Every swirl holds a promise anew,
As we blend our passions, watch them accrue.
Simmering slowly, the flavors combine,
Stirring with purpose, our dreams align.

A sprinkle of courage, a handful of grit,
In the kitchen of life, we never sit.
With hearts so bold, we shape our fate,
Stirring the pot, let's never wait.

For every challenge is a chance to bloom,
With purpose igniting from glimmers of gloom.
As we mix and we stir, together we'll rise,
Creating a feast under brightening skies.

So take up your spoon, let intentions unfold,
Stirring with purpose, let stories be told.
With unity strong, we'll savor the taste,
In this journey of life, there's no need for haste.

The Bake of Belonging

In a warm kitchen, we find our place,
Gathering together, hearts interlace.
Flour dust dances in soft morning light,
As we prepare for the joy of the night.

Yeast rises slowly, love folded in,
Creating a bond, where we all begin.
In the mix of our lives, each story is shared,
In the bake of belonging, we know we're prepared.

From diverse flavors, a harmony grows,
A rich tapestry of highs and lows.
With every layer, we come to see,
The beauty in sharing, just you and me.

So let's preheat our hearts with cheer,
As we bake together, dispelling all fear.
Tucking in kindness, love is the key,
In this bake of belonging, we set spirits free.

With golden crusts and sweet filling near,
We celebrate moments, the laughter, the cheer.
For in every bite, we find our home,
In the bake of belonging, together we roam.

Sauteed Moments of Clarity

A flicker of light, in the pan it breaks,
Chopped dreams sizzle, like waking stakes.
Each essence browned, a flavor awake,
In oil's embrace, clarity takes.

Steaming thoughts dance, in fragrant air,
With every stir, a memory laid bare.
Gathered whispers, a truth to share,
In this moment, we're free from care.

The heat of chaos, a guiding flame,
Transforming confusion, giving it name.
Each taste familiar, yet never the same,
In this saute, we find our claim.

Glimmers of wisdom, like herbs we toss,
In the mix, our fears embossed.
Stirring gently, we count the cost,
In this creation, we're never lost.

A plate of life, served warm and bright,
Moments of clarity, our shared delight.
With every bite, the future ignites,
Sauteed moments, shining light.

Whisked Together

In a bowl of dreams, we begin to blend,
Eggs and sugar, the sweet we send.
Whisked together, each heart to mend,
A frothy mix, where love won't end.

The rhythm of life, a steady spin,
Folding in hope, where joy begins.
Butter and laughter, the secret wins,
In this creation, our souls are twins.

Quiet moments, whisking slow,
The magic it takes, to rise and grow.
A pinch of patience, watch it flow,
In every swirl, the love we show.

Baking our past, in warmth we trust,
Golden edges, each bite a must.
With every taste, the flavors gust,
Whisked together, it's more than just.

A recipe shared, with stories told,
In every layer, memories unfold.
From simple ingredients, to treasures bold,
Whisked together, our hearts consoled.

Mutual Growth in Tenderness

In gentle soil, our roots entwine,
Nurtured by warmth, the sun's design.
A blooming trust, like vines that climb,
Together we flourish, in perfect time.

Through storms we bend, but never break,
The love we share, the steps we take.
Each new leaf, a bond awake,
In mutual growth, our hearts partake.

Patience we cultivate, day by day,
With every challenge, we find our way.
In tender moments, we learn to stay,
A garden of strength, come what may.

Seasons will change, but we are here,
In whispers soft, our dreams draw near.
Through laughter and tears, we persevere,
In mutual growth, our path is clear.

With hands entwined, we sow the seeds,
Of kindness, grace, and loving deeds.
In the garden of life, our spirit feeds,
Mutual growth, where every heart leads.

Feeding the Soul

In the quiet hour, we gather close,
A table set, our hearts engrossed.
Each bite shared, a warm dose,
Feeding the soul, like a whispered prose.

The laughter bubbles, like broth in pot,
In stories shared, we find our spot.
Every flavor tells, connects the dot,
Feeding the soul, it matters a lot.

A feast of colors, bright and bold,
Every dish served, a memory told.
In this communion, the warmth we hold,
Feeding the soul, a treasure of gold.

As twilight falls, we raise a glass,
To moments cherished, that never pass.
In every clink, our worries surpass,
Feeding the soul, as the shadows amass.

In the end, it's love that fills;
In every flavor, our heart distills.
Feeding the soul, our spirit thrills,
In shared meals, life's joy fulfills.

Created in Trust

In whispers soft, our bond began,
A silent pact, hand in hand.
Through trials deep and laughter bright,
In every shade, we find the light.

With every word, a promise made,
In shadows cast, our fears will fade.
We'll build a world, brick by brick,
In trust's embrace, our hearts will tick.

Moments shared, both big and small,
In every rise, together fall.
A gentle heart that knows the way,
Together stronger, come what may.

Through storms that rage and winds that howl,
We'll face the night, in strength, we growl.
For in this life, our roots run deep,
In trust we leap, in love we keep.

So let the world spin, let time flow,
In every tide, our love will grow.
In bonds unseen, we rise, we thrust,
Forever bound, we're created in trust.

Layers of Affection

In whispers warm, affection blooms,
Each layer deep, where silence looms.
With every glance, a story told,
In subtle shades, our hearts unfold.

Wrapped in moments, soft and sweet,
A gentle touch, our souls repeat.
With breathless laughs, and shared dreams,
In tender tones, our passion streams.

Like petals bright on morning dew,
In every layer, I find you.
Through seasons change, we stand as one,
In every shade, our love's begun.

With tiny gestures, everyday,
We build our fort, come what may.
The depth of love, it knows no bounds,
In layers rich, true beauty found.

Together we weave, in soft embrace,
Creating space, a sacred place.
With every sigh, our spirits blend,
In layers of affection, love won't end.

Tapestry of Togetherness

In threads of gold, our lives entwine,
Each moment shared is truly divine.
With colors bright, we craft our tale,
In unity strong, we shall not pale.

With hearts in sync, we dance as one,
In laughter bright, from dawn to sun.
The fabric of dreams, stitched with care,
In this embrace, nothing can compare.

Through trials faced and joys unveiled,
In every stitch, our love has sailed.
With every beat, our story grows,
In this soft weave, our spirit flows.

Together we gather, hand in hand,
In every thread, we make our stand.
A tapestry rich, with threads of fate,
In togetherness, we celebrate.

So let the loom spin, time unravel,
In every moment, together we travel.
With love as our guide, let's not sever,
In this tapestry, we are forever.

Nibbles of Joy

In simple bites, delight we find,
With laughter shared, hearts intertwined.
Each nibble small, a taste of glee,
In every crumb, sweet memories.

From cookies baked to moments shared,
In every flavor, joy declared.
With friends around, in sun or rain,
We savor life, in blissful grain.

Like whispers soft, a gentle tease,
Each nibble brings us to our knees.
In every morsel, laughter rings,
In joyous bites, our spirit sings.

Through meals prepared with tender care,
In every taste, love fills the air.
With every bite, let time stand still,
In nibbles of joy, our hearts to fill.

So gather close, let stories flow,
In every dish, let warmth bestow.
For in these moments, we deploy,
A banquet rich, with nibbles of joy.

Stirring the Pot of Love

In the kitchen, warmth embraced,
Two hearts mingling, sweetly laced.
A dash of spice, a pinch of care,
Together we create, a love we share.

Bubbling laughter, simmering dreams,
Stirring the pot, life's flowing streams.
Herbs of joy, a sprinkle of trust,
In this recipe, we find our lust.

A taste of memories, rich and bold,
Each secret stirred, a story told.
From savory whisks to gentle sighs,
In this dance of flavors, love never dies.

Chop and dice, with hands entwined,
In every slice, our hearts aligned.
As the broth thickens, our souls unite,
Stirring the pot, through day and night.

Together we simmer, together we feast,
In every bite, our joys released.
For love is the dish we cook so right,
Stirring the pot, our hearts ignite.

Shared Secrets and Silence

In whispers soft, we share our dreams,
Beneath the stars, where silence gleams.
Eyes meet softly, hearts reveal,
In this moment, love feels real.

Secrets hidden, wrapped in night,
Our laughter echoes, pure delight.
Silent promises dance on air,
In this hush, we lay ourselves bare.

The world around us fades away,
In this stillness, we softly sway.
A gentle touch, a knowing glance,
In shared secrets, we find our chance.

Beyond the noise, our voices blend,
In silence sweet, our souls defend.
Bound by trust, like shadows cast,
In whispered words, our hearts hold fast.

Together we walk, hand in hand,
In this quiet, we understand.
Shared secrets bloom like fragrant flowers,
In the silence, love empowers.

Savory Touches

A gentle brush, a fleeting kiss,
In every touch, I find my bliss.
Savory moments, rich and bold,
With every heartbeat, our story told.

Fingers linger, time stands still,
In your embrace, I find my will.
Spices of life in every caress,
In savory touches, we feel our best.

Caresses soft as morning dew,
With every taste, I crave for you.
The warmth between us, a cozy glow,
In these touches, our love will grow.

Wrap me close, don't let me go,
In this savor, let feelings flow.
Each kiss, a dish, crafted with care,
In savory touches, we lay ourselves bare.

For love's a feast, a glorious spread,
In every moment, our hearts are fed.
With flavors bursting, we uncover,
In savory touches, we cherish each other.

Slices of Laughter

In the evening glow, laughter rings,
Joyful moments, oh, the bliss it brings.
With every giggle, the shadows fade,
In slices of laughter, love is made.

Chop it finely, a dash of cheer,
Life tastes sweeter when you are near.
We share the jokes, and stories told,
In this recipe, our hearts unfold.

Slice by slice, we craft delight,
Building memories, gleaming bright.
Through every chuckle, joy ignites,
In this banquet, our spirit lights.

Gather around, let the good times flow,
Each slice a treasure, letting love grow.
In tasty morsels of humor shared,
In life's laughter, we feel prepared.

So here's to moments, light and free,
In slices of laughter, you and me.
Through every giggle, love takes flight,
In our hearts, we find the light.

Savory Silent Moments

In twilight's calm embrace we sit,
The world fades softly, a perfect fit.
A glance exchanged, warmth in the air,
In savory silence, we find our care.

Memories linger like spices sweet,
Each heartbeat dances, each moment replete.
Together we savor, the quiet delight,
In the hush of the evening, everything feels right.

Time stretches gently, like a soft-spun thread,
With whispered dreams and words unsaid.
Every tick of the clock seems to know,
In savory silence, our hearts gently flow.

When stars unveil their glimmering glow,
In silent moments, our love will grow.
Wrapped in your presence, I find my peace,
In the taste of stillness, all worries cease.

Through savory silent moments we drift,
In the space between words, we discover a gift.
Here in the quiet, our souls intertwine,
Creating a memory, both yours and mine.

Wholesome Whispers of Support

In the still of the night, a soft whisper grows,
Wrapped in warmth, like the sun's gentle glow.
A hand to hold, in the darkest of times,
Wholesome whispers, like melodies, chime.

With every word, a lifeline we weave,
In moments of doubt, together we believe.
Through trials and tears, we stand side by side,
In wholesome whispers, we become our guide.

The strength in your voice, a tender embrace,
Guiding me through, a warm, sacred place.
In laughter and sorrow, our spirits entwine,
Wholesome whispers support like the sweetest wine.

When shadows descend, and fears start to creep,
Your whispers remind me, love's promises keep.
A fortress of faith, we build with our care,
Together we flourish, through every despair.

In this bond, we rise like the dawn's bright light,
Wholesome whispers ignite hopes for the fight.
In the tapestry of life, our threads are so fine,
With whispers of support, our hearts intertwine.

Ingredients of Affection

A pinch of kindness, a dash of grace,
In every gesture, love leaves its trace.
From glances shared to laughter's embrace,
Ingredients of affection, life's warm base.

Stirred together, the heart learns to sing,
In simple moments, oh, the joy they bring.
Sprinkled with trust, love's flavors unfold,
Each taste savored, a story retold.

A recipe cherished, both tender and true,
Each ingredient crafted, just me and you.
Seasoned with time, our bonds grow strong,
In the kitchen of life, we dance to our song.

With each gentle stir, deeper connections arise,
The warmth of affection reflects in our eyes.
In the pot of our hearts, simmering slow,
Ingredients of affection, forever will glow.

In the dinner of life, may we always find,
A table set lovingly, with hearts intertwined.
Every day offers a chance to create,
With ingredients of affection, we celebrate fate.

Whispers of Understanding

In quiet corners, where shadows blend,
Whispers of understanding around us extend.
A gentle nod, a warm, knowing glance,
In unspoken moments, our souls take a chance.

Through storms of confusion, we find our way,
In the language of feeling, we choose to stay.
Listening close, with hearts open wide,
In whispers of understanding, we never must hide.

As seasons change, and paths intertwine,
In moments together, our spirits align.
With patience unmatched, we navigate fear,
Whispers of understanding make intentions clear.

Each word a bridge over rivers of doubt,
In the embrace of kindness, we learn what it's about.
In laughter, in silence, in sweet harmony,
Whispers of understanding paint us free.

As night settles down, and day starts to fade,
We cherish the bond that together we've made.
With whispers embraced, our fears will shatter,
For in understanding, we find what does matter.

Stirring Souls Together

In the quiet of the night,
We gather under stars bright.
Whispers dance, the air is light,
Stirring souls, hearts take flight.

Laughter flows like gentle streams,
In the fabric of our dreams.
Hand in hand, or so it seems,
Together we weave our themes.

Beneath the moon, secrets shared,
With every glance, love declared.
A tapestry of thoughts prepared,
In this space, no heart is scared.

Through the storms and through the calm,
We find a place, a healing balm.
In unity, we hold a psalm,
Stirring souls with endless charm.

As dawn arrives, we part our ways,
Yet in our hearts, forever stays.
A bond that time cannot erase,
Stirring souls, a warm embrace.

The Oven of Understanding

In the heat of the moment,
Compassion rises, we're potent.
We bake our thoughts till they're bent,
In the oven of understanding.

Ingredients are love and care,
Mixed with patience, sweet and rare.
Turning struggles into flair,
In this warmth, we truly share.

As the flames flicker and sway,
We savor truths in every way.
Creating bonds that gently stay,
In the oven where hearts play.

With every taste, we learn anew,
What it means to start and pursue.
Together, we shape the view,
In the oven, our love is true.

When the timer calls us near,
We find our hearts are crystal clear.
In this space, we lose all fear,
The oven whispers, "Love is here."

Ingredients of Affection

With a pinch of trust, we start,
A sprinkle of joy fills each heart.
Mix in kindness, a vital part,
Ingredients that never depart.

As we stir with gentle grace,
Laughter blooms in every space.
Moments shared, we interlace,
Cooking love at our own pace.

In the cauldron, dreams take form,
Through gentle hands, we keep it warm.
In unity, we brave the storm,
Ingredients of love transform.

Taste the sweetness in the air,
A recipe beyond compare.
In every glance, a tender care,
Affection's essence everywhere.

As the feast of life unfolds,
Each bite reflects the love we hold.
The ingredients of stories told,
In every heart, affection bold.

A Harmony of Hearts

In twilight's glow, we find our tune,
A serenade beneath the moon.
Each heartbeat plays a loving rune,
Creating rhythms sweet as June.

Voices rise like notes in air,
In every sound, we lose our care.
Together we blend, hearts laid bare,
A harmony beyond compare.

In the silence, a melody,
Unspoken words, a symphony.
Through gentle chords, we feel the spree,
In this dance of unity.

With each refrain, we intertwine,
A tapestry of hearts divine.
In every heartbeat, love does shine,
In harmony, our souls align.

As dreams and hopes in chorus swell,
We draw the light, we cast the spell.
In this space, all is farewell,
A harmony where love will dwell.

Nurtured by Vulnerability

In gentle whispers, fears take flight,
Hearts unfold in the waning light.
Courage blooms in tender care,
A bond formed in the open air.

Trust like petals, soft and bright,
Embraced by shadows of the night.
With every tear, a deeper thread,
In honest words, our spirits fed.

Together we dance through the unknown,
In the fragile spaces, love is grown.
In vulnerability, we find our strength,
A sacred journey, unmeasured length.

Each scar we share is painted gold,
A tapestry of stories told.
In openness, our hearts ignite,
A chorus hums, a shared delight.

Nurtured softly, we rise again,
In trust, we find a refuge, friend.
Through each storm, we learn to see,
In vulnerability, we are free.

Culinary Harmony of Hearts

In the kitchen where aromas blend,
Flavors dance, and hearts transcend.
Chopping onions, laughter flows,
A recipe born from love that grows.

Stirring pots with gentle grace,
Every meal, a warm embrace.
Spices mingle, stories shared,
In every taste, a life declared.

The clinking glasses, cheers abound,
In every bite, sweet joys are found.
Cooking side by side, hand in hand,
Creating love, a feast so grand.

Baking warmth in every loaf,
Savoring moments, hearts are both.
Ingredients of trust and care,
Culinary symphony, a love affair.

Together we share, a lasting spark,
In culinary harmony, we leave our mark.
Meals become memories, cherished and bright,
In the warmth of our kitchen, love's pure light.

Spices of Support

In every blend, a story lies,
Support given, it never dies.
A pinch of care, a dash of trust,
In life's grand recipe, it's a must.

Cinnamon hugs and ginger's grace,
In the kitchen of life, we find our place.
Each season brings a different spice,
Friendship's essence, warm and nice.

From hot pepper to soothing sage,
Through every challenge, we turn the page.
In moments bitter, we find the sweet,
With spices of support, our hearts compete.

Together we simmer through highs and lows,
In every challenge, our strength grows.
A flavorful journey, hand in hand,
In the banquet of life, together we stand.

Bringing warmth with every share,
Together, we spice the air.
With love as the base, we add and blend,
In the flavors of life, support won't end.

Melodies of Laughter

In joyful tunes, we find our way,
Laughter echoes, brightens the day.
Each chuckle shared, a note in the air,
In symphonies sweet, hearts lay bare.

A playful wink, a silly jest,
In every giggle, we are blessed.
Harmony found in smiles wide,
With laughter as lanterns, we feel alive.

Moments fleeting, treasured and pure,
In shared laughter, loves endure.
A chorus rising, spirits soar,
In melodies sweet, we crave for more.

Dancing through the trials, we sing,
Joyful heartbeats, laughter's spring.
With every note, a bond we weave,
In the melody, we truly believe.

Together we laugh, and time stands still,
In the music of joy, we find our thrill.
In every sound, our hearts align,
In these melodies, love will shine.

Balanced Hearts and Palates

In a world of flavors bright,
We find joy, pure delight.
Each bite tells a story true,
Binding hearts, me and you.

In harmony, we will dine,
With every course, your hand in mine.
Seasoned with laughter, trust, and grace,
Together, we embrace this space.

A sprinkle of love, a dash of care,
Creating moments, soul laid bare.
With plates aligned, our spirits soar,
Balanced hearts seek to explore.

From sweet to savory, a dance unfolds,
In every taste, our bond unfolds.
A symphony of rich delight,
In shared meals, we find our light.

Table of Togetherness

Gathered round, the table set,
With cherished friends, no regret.
In every laugh, in every toast,
Togetherness, we love the most.

Dishes clatter, stories flow,
Every moment, love will grow.
United in joy, we share our feast,
In this place, worries cease.

The warmth of candles flickering bright,
A circle formed, hearts taking flight.
From soup to dessert, flavors blend,
In this embrace, we find our friend.

Echoes of laughter fill the air,
Gathered close, we have no care.
In every bite, a memory made,
At this table, our hearts parade.

Fusion of Dreams

In a kitchen where dreams collide,
Cultures meet and flavors bide.
A pinch of hope, a splash of cheer,
Creating magic, far and near.

Each recipe, a tale unfolds,
Secret whispers of the bold.
With every stirring, passion flows,
As new horizons bloom and grow.

From spices old, to visions new,
Together we craft, me and you.
A fusion dance that knows no bounds,
In every dish, our heart resounds.

With every taste, a joy ignites,
A canvas painted with our bites.
In this journey, hand in hand,
We savor dreams, a loving strand.

Handcrafted Promises

Each meal a promise, lovingly made,
Crafted with care, never to fade.
Ingredients chosen, with heart and soul,
Together we make our spirits whole.

A recipe of laughter, a pinch of tears,
Binding us close through all the years.
Savor the moments, rich and deep,
In this space, our hearts we keep.

Kneading dough, like shaping fate,
In every rise, we celebrate.
With every serving, bonds renew,
In this banquet, love shines through.

From simmering pots to baked delight,
Each handcrafted dish feels just right.
Under the stars, our tales we share,
In promises echoing, we lay bare.

Spices of Shared Secrets

In whispers shared, we mix and blend,
The flavors of trust, a journey's end.
Cinnamon tales and nutmeg dreams,
A recipe stitched through silent seams.

With every pinch, our stories rise,
Seasoned with laughter, joy in our eyes.
A dash of hope, a sprinkle of grace,
Together we savor this sacred space.

In the warmth of hearts, the pot does simmer,
As secrets dance, our souls grow dimmer.
Each note we share, a flavor divine,
In the spices of life, our spirits entwine.

Beneath the stars, our dishes glow,
A banquet of truths, we ebb and flow.
In the quiet hum of a quiet night,
We feast on dreams, in shared delight.

These spices of life, forever we'll hold,
In memories cherished, our stories bold.
A tapestry woven with love and care,
In the kitchen of trust, we gather and share.

Baking Memories in the Sun

Under the sun, we gather near,
Mixing our laughter, hearts full of cheer.
Flour dust dances in golden light,
As we create, our spirits take flight.

Ovens warm, with love they glow,
Cookies of joy, in each warm flow.
With every stir, we craft our dreams,
Baking together, nothing's as it seems.

Rolling dough, with hands intertwined,
Moments we make, peaceful and kind.
Sugar and spice, in every bite,
Memories rising, pure and bright.

The scent of vanilla fills the air,
A promise of sweetness, love everywhere.
In the warmth of the sun, we share and create,
Baking our memories, it's never too late.

As shadows stretch long, laughter will reign,
In every crumb, we will sustain.
Baking together, a bond so strong,
In the joy of the moment, we all belong.

Kneading Love with Laughter

With hands in dough, we shape our fate,
Kneading in love, it's never too late.
Laughter flows freely, a rhythm we find,
In every fold, our hearts are aligned.

The yeast of our friendship begins to rise,
Warmth in the kitchen, joy in our eyes.
Sprinkling flour, like stars in the night,
Kneading together, our bond feels right.

With every push, our worries release,
In the dough we mold, there's comfort and peace.
A pinch of laughter, a sprinkle of care,
Creating our future, together we dare.

The oven's warmth embraces us tight,
As love bakes, we bask in the light.
Golden crusts tell tales of our days,
In every bite, love's soft gaze.

As we share our feast, hearts open wide,
In kneaded delights, our dreams will abide.
Together forever, through laughter and strife,
Kneading our love, the recipe of life.

Mixing Differences and Similarities

In a pot of life, we stir and swirl,
Flavors distinct, a vibrant world.
Salt and sugar, a dance of fate,
In every contrast, we learn to create.

Dashing of spice, a blend unique,
In differences found, our voices speak.
Bold ingredients, we freely embrace,
Together a feast, in this shared space.

As cultures collide, new dishes arise,
A palette of stories, sweet surprise.
With each new taste, we find our song,
In mixing it up, we truly belong.

Serving together, our table diverse,
A banquet of life, our flavors converse.
In unity found, our hearts intertwine,
Mixing our differences, all will be fine.

Together we savor, together we learn,
In every bite, new friendships we earn.
Celebrating us, in every way,
Mixing life's flavors, brightening the day.

Morsels of Memories

In the quiet of twilight's embrace,
We gather moments, time cannot erase.
Whispers of laughter, echoes of cheer,
Taste of nostalgia, always so near.

Faded photographs, sepia tone,
Stories unspooled, seeds we have sown.
Fingers recall each texture and hue,
Morsels of moments shared between you.

The scent of the kitchen, aromas that blend,
Capturing time, where beginnings transcend.
A table adorned with love's gentle grace,
Each dish a reminder, a cherished place.

Songs of the past, a sweet serenade,
Dancing on tongues, memories replayed.
In bites so tender, we savor the taste,
Morsels of memories, no moment to waste.

Gathered together, we share tales anew,
Each morsel a blessing, each flavor rings true.
In every small serving, a life intertwined,
Morsels of memories, forever enshrined.

A Garden of Growth and Giving

In a garden of blooms, where dreams can sprout,
Roots intertwine, of that there's no doubt.
Sunshine and rain, the balance of grace,
Each tender shoot finds its rightful place.

Seeds of compassion, sown into ground,
Flourishing hearts, with love they are bound.
Nurtured by kindness, they reach for the sky,
In this garden of giving, hopes shall not die.

Colorful petals, adorned with the morn,
Harvest of care, in new life reborn.
With every season, the circle persists,
In a garden of growth, no love is missed.

Together we toil, hands dirty and free,
Creating a haven, for you and for me.
A tapestry woven, in sunlight and rain,
In a garden of giving, we thrive without pain.

Through toil and patience, we learn and we grow,
In the warmth of the sun, our spirits will flow.
Each blossom a promise, each vine a sweet tale,
In this garden of growth, together we sail.

Fermenting Futures

In barrels of dreams, our futures await,
Time gently alters, as flavors create.
Yeast of our hopes, bubbling with cheer,
Fermenting ideas, both far and near.

The rush of ambition, a heady delight,
Turning sweet wishes to visions in flight.
Patience is key in this delicate art,
As we blend our passions, making them start.

A sprinkle of laughter, a dash of despair,
Collective experiences, we willingly share.
With every new twist in this swirling brew,
Fermenting our future, the old and the new.

We'll gather the stories, rich and diverse,
Stirring together, we'll break the curse.
Lives intertwined, like vines in a row,
In fermenting futures, together we grow.

Here in this process, our spirits align,
Transforming our thoughts, like grapes into wine.
With hope as our harvest, the future's our prize,
Fermenting our fates, under kind, watchful skies.

Taste Testing Trials and Triumphs

In a kitchen alive, with flavors galore,
We dive into trials, discovering more.
With each bite of courage, we learn and we grow,
Taste testing life, embracing the flow.

Failures are lessons, sweet victories too,
A pinch of resilience in all that we do.
From burning the edges to flavors just right,
We savor the journey, through day and through night.

Each ingredient gathered, like stories we tell,
A dash of adventure, a sprinkle of hell.
As palates evolve, we uncover our souls,
Taste testing trials, as each moment unfolds.

With friends by our side, we feast on our fate,
In laughter and love, we tempt every plate.
Through trials and triumphs, we forge our own way,
In taste testing life, we find joy every day.

Together we offer, our best to the feast,
A banquet of memories, joys never ceased.
With forks held high, we embrace what we share,
Taste testing trials, with flavors so rare.

Relishing Each Chapter

In pages worn, stories unfold,
Time whispers tales, both new and old.
Each sentence a savor, each word a bite,
We relish the journey, from day to night.

With laughter and tears, we turn the page,
Life's lessons learned at every stage.
In binding of memories, we find our place,
Embracing the moments, we shall not erase.

A vibrant world in black and white,
Colors ignite when we read with delight.
We dive into dreams, step into the lore,
Each chapter penned opens a door.

As characters dance through the inked line,
We find our own stories in every sign.
In these bound tomes, our lives intertwine,
Relishing the chapters, one foot in time.

Unity in Diversity

In colors bright, the world does sing,
Harmony blooms, diversity's wing.
Voices unite in a vibrant embrace,
Together we stand, in every place.

Each culture a thread in a beautiful seam,
Woven with care, like a shared dream.
Hand in hand, we rise and create,
Unity blossoms, diverse and great.

From mountains high to valleys low,
Embracing the stories that freely flow.
In laughter and joy, our spirits aligned,
Finding connection in hearts intertwined.

Differences cherished, each tale we tell,
In this grand tapestry, we all dwell.
With open hearts and minds, we see,
That unity thrives in diversity.

Let us celebrate with dance and song,
In every heartbeat, we all belong.
Together we flourish, together we rise,
In the beauty of life, our love never dies.

A Flavorful Odyssey

From spice-laden streets to quiet cafes,
Every bite tells of distant days.
A world on a plate, flavors collide,
In kitchens of love, where dreams reside.

The sizzle of garlic, the zest of lime,
Each morsel awakens the sense of time.
With every dish, a journey unfolds,
Tales of tradition, eager to be told.

Savory, sweet, or tangy delight,
The palette dances, a feast in sight.
From faraway lands to home-cooked grace,
In every flavor, we discover our place.

We gather around, sharing stories and cheer,
In meals we bond, bringing hearts near.
Savoring cultures on our eager tongues,
An odyssey crafted, where joy belongs.

So lift your glass, toast to the night,
In this culinary journey, take flight.
For every meal shared is a treasure found,
A flavorful odyssey, where love abounds.

Hearty Conversations

In quiet corners, voices rise,
Words woven gently beneath the skies.
With laughter and wisdom, hearts unfold,
In the warmth of stories, we find our gold.

Each dialogue crafted, a tapestry spun,
Emotions shared, two souls become one.
From whispers of dreams to echoes of fears,
Hearty conversations bring smiles and tears.

We dive into moments, both light and deep,
In open discourse, connections we keep.
Through questions and musings, we learn and grow,
Like rivers that flow, our spirits bestow.

With every exchange, a bridge we build,
Understanding deepens, our hearts are filled.
In the art of talking, we find our way,
Hearty conversations, brightening the day.

So gather close, let the words take flight,
In shared reflections, we shine our light.
For in every chat lies a love that thrives,
Hearty conversations, where true life derives.

Moments of Tender Preparation

In the quiet dawn, we gather near,
Whispers of love, the heart can hear.
With gentle hands, the table we lay,
A feast of memories, come what may.

Chopping and stirring, scents fill the air,
Laughter dances, dispelling all care.
Each ingredient holds a story to share,
In moments of preparation, we show we care.

As pots simmer softly, conversations flow,
Time stands still, in warmth we grow.
Every glance shared, a promise we keep,
In tender moments, our souls we steep.

With every tick of the clock, hearts unite,
In the magic of cooking, everything's right.
So here we stand, as one, side by side,
In moments of joy, our love won't hide.

The table adorned with laughter and cheer,
Holding our dreams, both far and near.
Moments like this, forever reside,
In the chambers of love, where hopes abide.

The Feast of Understanding

Gather together, let voices blend,
In this feast, our hearts we send.
Each dish served tells a tale so sweet,
A tapestry woven, each thread a treat.

With every bite, we savor the past,
Moments we cherish, forever to last.
In laughter and stories, our spirits soar,
Around this table, we learn to explore.

The warmth of connection fills up the room,
Like flowers in bloom, dispelling all gloom.
With every glance, we find common ground,
In this feast of understanding, love is found.

With spices of trust, and sauces of grace,
We carve out the night, our own special place.
In silence, we hold the truths we know,
In each heart's language, feelings grow.

And when the last bite is joyfully shared,
In the echo of laughter, we know we've dared.
To feast on the moments, both gentle and grand,
United in spirit, together we stand.

Savory Journeys

Step into the kitchen, adventures await,
With fragrant aromas, we tempt our fate.
Each journey begins with pots and pans,
Together we roam to faraway lands.

Through spices we travel, across ocean blue,
A pinch of this and a dash of that too.
With spatulas ready, we rise to the call,
In savory journeys, we'll conquer it all.

From deserts so hot to mountains so high,
Every dish tells tales, let's give it a try.
With flavors that dance, our hearts take flight,
In savory journeys, we shine ever bright.

With every new taste, a story unfolds,
From herbs of the earth to treasures of gold.
In laughter unyielding, we mix and we mold,
In savory journeys, our dreams we hold.

So lift your glass high, let's toast to the night,
To journeys we share, to flavors so right.
Through every adventure, our spirits embrace,
In the kitchen of life, we find our place.

Cupfuls of Care

Warm greetings gather, with hugs to begin,
A cupful of care, our friendship within.
With each gentle sip, warmth fills the air,
In simple moments, true love lays bare.

Tea brewed with kindness, a sprinkle of joy,
A recipe cherished, not just a ploy.
With biscuits beside, laughter takes flight,
In cupfuls of care, the world feels right.

Conversations flow like honey and thyme,
We savor each word, every rhythm, each rhyme.
In the comfort of company, hearts intertwine,
In cupfuls of care, our spirits align.

So let's gather 'round, with stories to share,
Each moment enveloped in love and in care.
From the smallest of cups, to memories vast,
In cupfuls of care, our bond will hold fast.

As daylight fades softly, we linger on,
In the warmth of connection, we've all truly won.
With every shared smile and each knowing glance,
In cupfuls of care, we seize every chance.

Aroma of Memories

The scent of bread in the air,
Whispers of laughter everywhere.
A kitchen bathed in warm light,
Memories dance in the night.

Spices mingle, flavors collide,
An old cookbook, our trusted guide.
Each page turned sparks a smile,
Moments cherished, all the while.

Baking cookies with a friend,
Sweet delights that never end.
Warmth that fills the heart and soul,
Aroma wraps us, makes us whole.

The simmering pot, a sacred sound,
In every drop, love is found.
A touch of salt, a hint of thyme,
In every meal, a taste of time.

As candles flicker on the shelf,
We gather close, just being ourselves.
Aroma drifts, memories ignite,
In this space, everything feels right.

Tales of Time Together

Under the stars, we share our dreams,
Moonlight dances, softly gleams.
Stories woven like threads of gold,
Tales of love and courage bold.

With every laugh, the world feels wide,
Together, we turn the tide.
Friendship's warmth, a guiding star,
No matter where, we've come so far.

Through trials faced, we've grown strong,
In each other's hearts, we belong.
Lessons learned, paths intertwined,
In every moment, memories bind.

Sunsets painted in hues of red,
Words of comfort, softly said.
Gathered close, we feel the glow,
In this time, our spirits flow.

The chapters turn, yet love remains,
Through laughter, joy, and even pains.
Together we run, together we fly,
In these tales, we'll never say goodbye.

Cherished Ingredients

A pinch of love, a sprinkle of grace,
In every meal, a warm embrace.
Flour dusted on the kitchen floor,
Ingredients we can't ignore.

Tomatoes ripe and basil fresh,
Each taste brings a happy mesh.
Slow-cooked stews, aromas blend,
In every dish, traditions mend.

Gathered 'round, we break the bread,
Conversations bloom, stories spread.
Secrets shared in every bite,
Cherished moments, pure delight.

From grandma's touch to our own flair,
Cooking becomes a loving care.
Recipes handed down through time,
In every flavor, love will rhyme.

With every meal, our hearts connect,
The flavors linger and reflect.
Cherished ingredients, warm and true,
In every taste, it's me and you.

Recipes of Resilience

Life's ingredients, both rough and sweet,
Mixing courage when we face defeat.
A dash of hope, a sprinkle of cheer,
Recipes crafted through every fear.

Stirring storms, but we won't break,
In every trial, we learn to take.
A cup of strength, a spoon of trust,
In every challenge, we find we must.

From bitter moments, wisdom grows,
In the oven, love's warmth flows.
Timing matters when life's askew,
In our resilience, we renew.

Baking dreams from the ashes rise,
With every setback, we break the ties.
Together we stand, stronger each day,
With recipes guiding us on our way.

Through thick and thin, we gather near,
Sharing our hopes, conquering fear.
In every bite, the taste of fight,
Recipes of resilience, pure delight.

Bonds Brewed in Kindness

In whispers soft, we share our dreams,
With smiles that shine like moonlit beams.
A hand to hold when shadows creep,
In kindness sown, our hearts take leap.

With each small gesture, trust is grown,
Through laughter's light, we're never alone.
Together we rise, in joy we bask,
The ties we forge, a loving task.

Through storms we weather, side by side,
In every tear, love will abide.
With open hearts, we brave the night,
For kindness blooms, a guiding light.

In every moment, grace prevails,
In kindness offered, hope entails.
As bonds are brewed in shared refrain,
We weave our stories, joy and pain.

In laughter's echo, hearts collide,
With every hug, we turn the tide.
A tapestry of love we weave,
In bonds of kindness, we believe.

Heartstrings Entwined

In twilight's glow, our spirits dance,
With fleeting glances, fate's sweet chance.
Two laughter's rings, a soft embrace,
Entwined together, time can't erase.

Through whispered dreams and midnight calls,
In every heartbeat, love enthralls.
A silent promise in your eyes,
In shared moments, our spirits rise.

With hands held tight, we face the storm,
In every challenge, love transforms.
Through tangled paths, we find our way,
In heartstrings bound, we choose to stay.

In joy and sorrow, we remain,
Each chapter written, love's sweet gain.
In every glance, a story told,
As heartstrings play, our love is bold.

In gentle breaths, a rhythm flows,
With each connection, deeper grows.
In harmony, we find our place,
Two souls entwined by love's embrace.

Simmering Empathy

In quiet moments, we sit and share,
Each silent struggle met with care.
A gentle nod, a knowing glance,
In empathy lived, hearts start to dance.

With every story, we bridge the space,
In warmth, we find a sacred place.
A soft embrace to ease the pain,
In simmering empathy, love will reign.

Through layers peeled, our truths unfold,
In understanding, we are consoled.
Each unspoken word builds the thread,
In hearts alight, no words are said.

In struggles shared, our burdens lift,
A bond that's forged, a precious gift.
With every heartbeat, we redefine,
In simmering love, our souls align.

In shadows bright, a spark ignites,
Through empathy's lens, we find the lights.
Together we stand, against the tide,
In the warmth of love, we will abide.

A Dash of Patience

In gardens grown with gentle hands,
A dash of patience, love withstands.
With every bud, we learn to see,
The beauty blossoming, wild and free.

Through seasons change, we wait and trust,
In tender moments, love is a must.
With every trial, we learn to care,
With patience sweet, our hearts will dare.

In shifting tides, we find our way,
With quiet strength, we greet the day.
A measured step, a cherished breeze,
In patience held, our spirits ease.

Through trials faced, we grow in grace,
In each slow turn, we find our place.
With courage drawn from deep inside,
In a dash of patience, love will guide.

As time unwinds, our roots go deep,
In tranquil moments, dreams we keep.
With every heartbeat, we unfold,
A dash of patience, a tale retold.

Milton Keynes UK
Ingram Content Group UK Ltd.
UKHW022049111124
451035UK00014B/1030

9 789916 867655